# HOW TO REMEMBER NAMES:

## A MENTALIST'S GUIDE TO REMEMBERING THE NAMES AND FACES OF EVERYONE YOU MEET

KEVIN VINER

ISBN: 979-8-9862347-0-0 (Paperback edition)

ISBN: 979-8-9862347-1-7 (eBook edition)

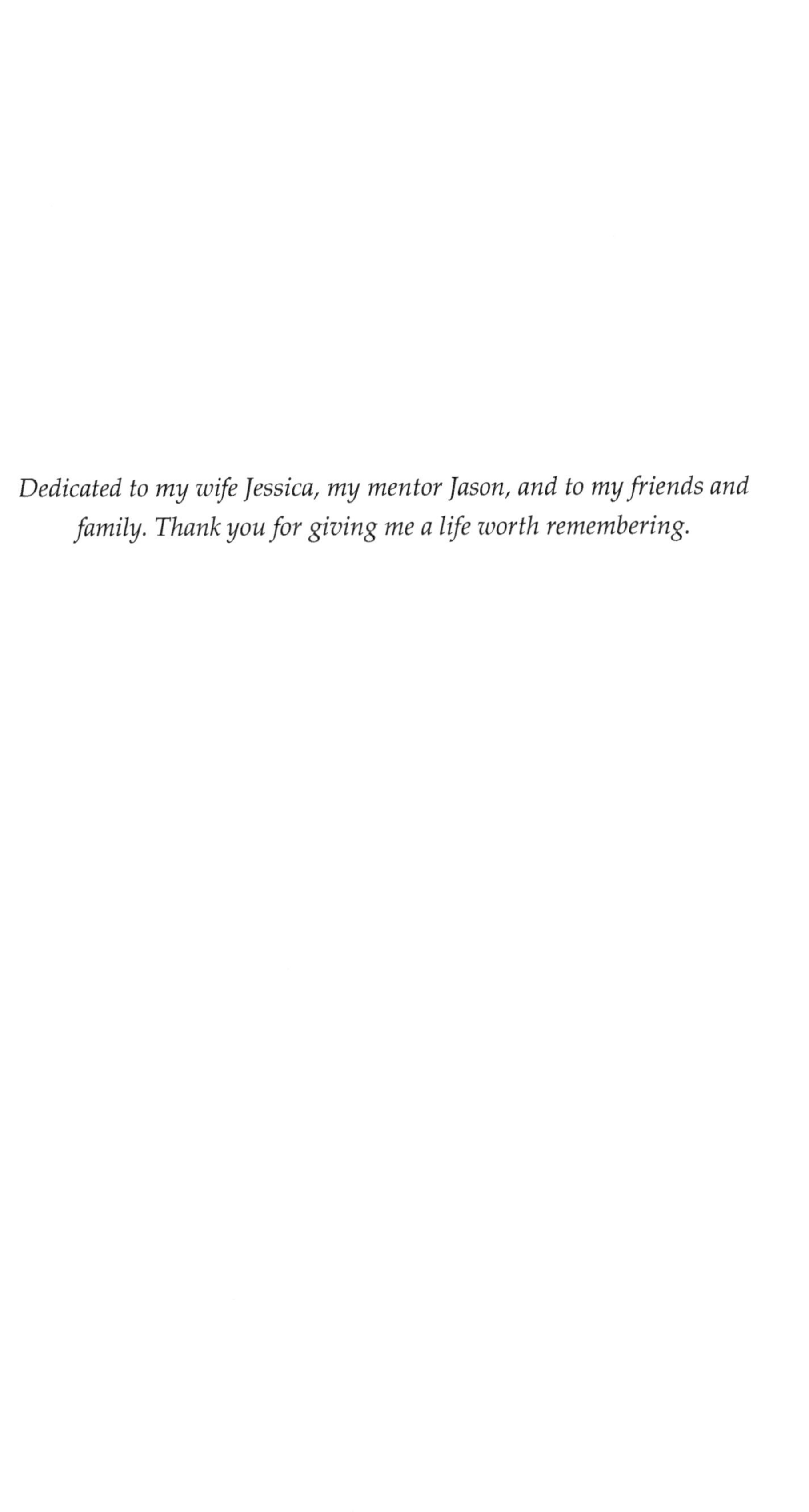


*Dedicated to my wife Jessica, my mentor Jason, and to my friends and family. Thank you for giving me a life worth remembering.*

# BONUS CONTENT

Access special bonus content at
https://kevinviner.net/remember-names/,
or by scanning the QR code below.

# CONTENTS

# INTRODUCTION



We've all had the experience of looking at somebody mid-conversation and sheepishly saying, "I'm sorry, what was your name?" Or hoping in vain that it will suddenly pop up in conversation (just a tip, it won't). Maybe you've experienced the awkwardness of somebody leaving a conversation saying, "Nice to meet you, Bob," and all you can respond with is, "You too!" while *you* know that *they* know that you forgot their name.

Relationships are the pillars that support our personal and business successes, and nothing builds trust and rapport faster than remembering people's names.

In my mid-twenties, I was speaking at a networking event that booked a musician to play some covers and original tunes. After her set, we wound up speaking to each other for the better part of an hour. Working up my courage, I asked if I might be able to take her out sometime. She said, "If you still know my name, I'll give you my number."

Jessica and I married each other three years later.

⁘

As a child, I was very interested in learning magic. This interest led to a full-time career as a mentalist, which is basically a magician who pretends to read minds. Whereas magicians focus on perfecting sleight-of-hand, the mentalist's toolbox contains methods built on psychology, mathematics, and a trained memory.

In a mentalism demonstration, cerebral gymnastics augment the performer's covert sleight of hand. The performer must remember facts about audience members, mentally cataloging and organizing multiple pieces of information that will be revealed much later in the show.

Regularly, audience members approach me after a show to ask if I have a photographic memory, and I let them know that my natural memory isn't anything special. In fact, eidetic memory (the scientific term for photographic memory) is largely considered a myth amongst neurologists and psychologists. The closest thing is a phenomenon called Highly Superior Autobiographical Memory (HSAM), thought to be experienced by fewer than 100 people around the world. I am certainly not one of them.

Fortunately, you won't be confined to your natural memory when you have the right tools at your disposal. In introductory physics, you may recall learning about how fulcrum placement can allow you to lift a heavy object with minimal force. Similarly, the tools that I give you in this book will allow you to appear to have a superhuman memory by exerting the right mental force in the right direction.

When I was 12 years old, I stumbled on *The Memory Book,* aptly named and written by the odd combination of magician turned memory expert Harry Lorayne and 1960s NBA star Jerry Lucas.

I was instantly hooked. While my friends were reading the latest *Hardy Boys* or *Goosebumps* books, I felt like Peter Parker discovering his spider powers. I was learning a new set of exciting tools that cracked the code to remembering anything I wanted. By using memory tricks called mnemonics (Greek for "relating to memory") to pair words with their definitions, I scored nearly perfectly on the vocabulary section of my SATs in high school. Similarly, I created acronyms and associations between instruments and their functions to pass my private and instrument pilot exams, and I regularly use these techniques for more mundane tasks like memorizing grocery lists.

You've used memory tricks in your own learning. If you recall the acronym PEMDAS for remembering the order of operations in mathematics, the name Roy G Biv for remembering the colors of the rainbow, or the phrase "Every Good Boy Does Fine" to remember the lines on a sheet music staff, you know how helpful these tools can be for learning new information.

The simple techniques in the following pages have transformed my life and my learning, freeing up time and mental space to work on the things I really enjoy. Gone are the days of worrying about what I will or won't remember. Now it's time to start *your* journey toward developing a superpower memory. Let's begin.

# CHAPTER 1

# IF YOU COULD ONLY DO ONE THING

People want solutions as quickly as possible, but with memorizing names, there is only so much that you can do instantly. With that said, the one piece of advice that will have the most impact is . . .

INTEND TO REMEMBER NAMES!

Sound self-explanatory? Not so fast. During college, I made my living by performing close-up magic at private events. I would walk in with a deck of cards and try to perform for every guest at the party as they socialized. Around the same time, I met a polymath and professional magician named Jason Randal, who graciously began to mentor me. During one of our many discussions, Jason asked me why people have me at their events.

"To fool their guests?"
Nope!

"To do card tricks?"
Wrong again.

We went down this path for a while until he finally gave me the answer. My job as an entertainer was to change the way that people feel, and magic was only the vehicle. He told me that most magicians show up with the intent to fool their audiences, and that's exactly what they do. But that's ALL they do.

He taught me that if I showed up with the intent to be an ambassador of goodwill, to really AFFECT the guests in a positive manner, I could still deliver on the fooling part while bringing much more to the table. If I endeavored to make a real connection with each guest while entertaining them, I could really transform their evening. Conversely, if I didn't show up intending to make a real connection, I likely wouldn't. As Andrea Bocelli said, "All that counts in life is intention."

Much like elevating the mood at party, memorizing names requires that you have the right INTENT. Showing up at a party and letting the names go in one ear and out the other is akin to running onto a baseball field without a glove. You've lost the war before starting the battle. Without intending to memorize names, you are unlikely to do so.

When you go for a jog, what's the first thing you do? You probably put on workout clothes and running shoes. When people struggle to exercise, behavioral psychologists have found that it makes a huge difference when people lay out workout clothes near their beds. When somebody wakes up and gets dressed to work out, they are much more likely to follow through. Their clothes give them a purpose. They have primed their brains and removed a barrier to entry.

So next time you go to an event, add a small reminder to your calendar that part of your purpose that evening will be to remember names. If you show up without the right intent, you are leaving it to chance that you will succeed. You might remember the names of people you meet, or you might not. If you show up intending to remember more names than you would normally, you will at least be more likely to succeed.

Of course, to fully utilize the skills in this book, you will need a bit more than just intent. You'll also need to practice. These skills are akin to learning an instrument, how to ride a bicycle, or how to type. There is an upfront effort that is required, but once the skill set is mastered, it is something that you will hang onto forever. Eventually, you will do these things naturally in your day-to-day conversations, and remembering names will become effortless.

# CHAPTER 2
## A PRIMER ON MEMORY

As a child, I loved *The Neverending Story* films. In *The Neverending Story 2*, the villain creates a machine that strips people of their memories, which are represented as singular crystal balls. This is how most of us think about our memories. We imagine that when we remember something, the entire memory is pulled as a whole from an internal catalog to the forefront of our brain. While this seems logical, it couldn't be further from the truth.

Recalling events from our past relies on what is called *episodic memory* (memories about specific moments). This is different from *semantic memory* (used for random facts and history) and *procedural memory* (how to do things, like riding a bike). Each time we remember something, we construct the story from various parts of our brains, and small errors creep in.

Over enough retellings of the story, certain elements stay and certain elements leave, and what we are left with becomes encoded. These "facts" become the stories we tell, even though the memories are often flawed. If you've ever stumbled upon an old journal, you may have experienced looking back on a memory and seeing that what actually happened is far different than what you have recalled. It's the same reason that eyewitness testimony is so problematic. Humans are naturally terrible at keeping mental records. That's why we rely so much on the written word.

Our *working memory* (short-term memory) can only hold about seven pieces of information at a time, and the latest research shows that anything above six pieces is a stretch for most. How do we overcome this and become superhuman at memorizing names?

The general principle involves using a mnemonic aid. Think of a mnemonic as a piece of information that acts as a bridge to something else. Every time we encode a memory, we essentially place a book randomly on a library shelf. We need a way to find the book later if we want to read it again. If you recall the Dewey Decimal System, you'll know that it is a classification system created by libraries to find any book on the shelf. When I was a child, I would always head to section 793.8 for the magic books. If you aren't a magician, that number means nothing to you. You need context.

Items lacking context are notoriously difficult to remember, and you are stuck only with your *rote memory* (memory through repetition), which may be how you remembered everything in elementary school. This book is all about bypassing your rote memory when working with names.

We create these mnemonic bridges through association. If you meet somebody named Rob, you could immediately create a mental image tying them somehow to "rob" ... maybe they are robbing a bank? Maybe they robbed you of your wallet? By creating this image, you increase your chance of later recalling that name.

Now you may be thinking to yourself, "Why would I want to add a step when I'm already struggling to remember names?" If you reflect on the names that you remember with ease, you may realize that you already do this. Imagine that you have a brother named Austin. Your first thought when you meet another Austin is, "That will be easy to remember. He shares my brother's name!" Your brother is now the bridge, and when you see that person, you are able to link them to something easy to remember (your brother), rather than an intangible piece of information.

This whole book is about enhancing things that you already do and teaching you how to create these bridges more efficiently. Memorizing names comes down to three basic steps, which I call *The 3Cs*, and after practicing the system for just a bit of time, you'll find that it begins to happen naturally. Even if it feels a bit odd at the beginning, that's okay! Increasing your memory by even twenty percent is a great start, and as a bonus, you'll be unlocking some of your natural creativity at the same time.

# CHAPTER 3
# THE SYSTEM: THE 3CS

The system for remembering names isn't very complicated. You'll do the exact same three things, in the exact same order, each and every time. It's as easy as "The 3Cs."

**C1. Create a CARICATURE**
**C2. Choose a CODE Word**
**C3. CHANGE the Person**

That's it in a nutshell. It isn't particularly difficult, and I'll explain the bare bones in the next few pages before we dive in deeper. For now, let's start with a specific example. Look at the picture below and imagine that this person is named Adam.

When you look at Adam, what do you notice first?

Most people tend to have a facial feature that is memorable or easily recognizable. Think of this as what an artist might accentuate in a CARICATURE or cartoon of the person. In Adam's case, I would notice his beard, especially since it is so long and pronounced.

The first thing we do is notice the beard and identify it as the outstanding feature. Now that we've done that, we get to choose a CODE WORD, which is the bridge we use to get us to Adam. My code word for every Adam I meet is "apple." You can think of Adam and Eve and the apple from the Garden of Eden, or more simply, of an "Adam's Apple."

Now you need to CHANGE them somehow by affecting them with your code word. In this case, we are pretending that his beard hangs so low because of the number of apples hiding inside of it. Or maybe he works for Apple secretly! Our new image of Adam might be something like this:

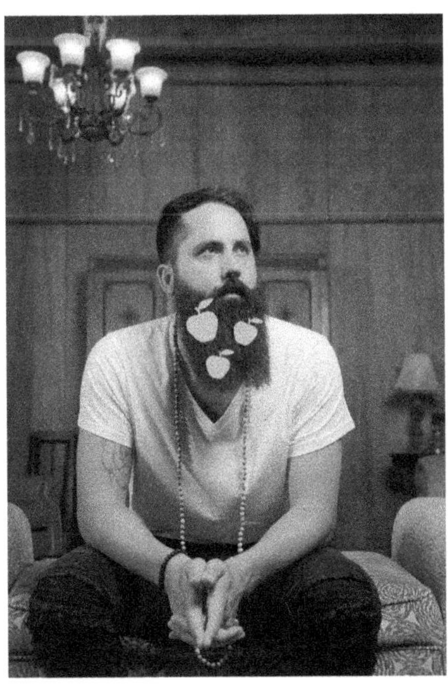

How is this helpful? Well, when we see Adam next, we will see his beard, which will trigger the image we made with the apples, and the apples will lead us right back to the name Adam. Every time we meet an Adam, we will pick a CARICATURE feature, choose the CODE WORD apple, and CHANGE that feature with the apples somehow.

Why does this work so well? We remember pictures far better than words. Psychologists call this the *picture superiority effect*. This is why savvy marketers present fancy infographics rather than just explaining their product. We remember the images better than any words they could present to us. Even in novels, the best authors work hard to use illustrative language so that we create pictures in our mind's eye.

Essentially, using **The 3Cs** forces us to convert information from something intangible (a name) to something that we can visualize.

Any system is only as good as its weakest link, and there are two primary places where I see people struggle when learning to remember names. The first involves not knowing the code words inside and out, which is something we will discuss at length. The second is simply that many people never take the time to apply the system.

Most of us show up at an event or a meeting with a million other things on our minds. "Did I wear the right thing?" "What will the partners at the company think about me?" "Will they like my pitch?" The last thing on our minds is remembering people's names, and thus they go in one ear and out the other.

Next time you step out to a dinner with new friends, to a networking event, or to meet the new hires, it's imperative that you create the right mindset and tell yourself that you WILL remember everybody's name that you meet. This is less about self-affirmation and more about priming yourself with the proper intent.

Set a simple goal for the evening, keeping in mind that this goal will evolve as you get more comfortable with the techniques. If you aim to remember the name of everybody in the room on your first attempt, you may get poor results and give up. But if you only attempt to remember three to four new names, you will gain the confidence to memorize more at the next go-around. We get better at the things we work at, plain and simple. So it shouldn't come as a surprise to you that you will need to do things a bit differently.

The first thing that you can do is give yourself every opportunity to get ahead. Back in the 1990s, a news reporter was interviewing Siegfried & Roy, at the time the highest-paid and most-lauded magicians in the world. When the reporter asked how the two met, Roy looked at Siegfried and laughed, saying, "Siegfried, apparently they haven't done their homework!" That question had been asked in so many interviews that the duo didn't feel like it merited their time. Talk show hosts and reporters excel at their jobs by researching their interviewees and finding the right questions to provide compelling interviews. They do their homework.

At your next event, make sure to do YOUR homework. If you attend a wedding, look over the names of the people sitting at your table and take a moment to familiarize yourself. If you have already memorized the code words for the names, think them through for a moment. Similarly, many corporate meetings use name badges to identify guests. If you are approaching a group cold, take a moment to look over the names before you walk up. An extra few seconds of time spent actively focusing can be the difference between disaster and success. It also ensures that you aren't seeing the names for the first time, in real time.

When a pilot works toward their instrument rating, they train to fly through clouds, where visibility is often zero. They rely solely on their instruments. Once the pilot understands their instruments, this isn't particularly difficult. This must be rehearsed until the mechanics are second nature, and the pilot knows the steps to follow inside and out. Only then can all mental power be spent following the instruments rather than figuring out how to interpret them.

Similarly, if you are seeing names for the first time and trying to memorize them simultaneously, it may prove difficult. By reviewing a guest list, reading name badges, or looking up conference attendees on LinkedIn prior to arrival, you can give yourself a leg up that might make all the difference.

## WHEN YOU MEET SOMEONE

When you meet somebody for the first time, LISTEN! There is a marked difference between hearing a name and absorbing the name into your mind. Memorizing names requires the latter. Actively repeat people's names back to them, and then repeat the name internally. Don't let the tray-passed hors d'oeuvres become a distraction! One of my mentalist superpowers is observation. As the saying goes, we were given two ears and one mouth so that we can listen twice as much as we speak.

# CHAPTER 4

# C1: CREATE A CARICATURE

Artificial intelligence does a great job at mimicking reality. Deep-fake technology can create a computerized vocal track that sounds like one of our favorite singers or even fabricate videos of our favorite celebrities. The BBC found itself in a bit of hot water in 2020 after creating a fake Christmas message from the late Queen Elizabeth II. Even though it was touted as fictitious by the network, people were concerned at just how convincing it looked.

As good as computers are at mimicking reality, they still struggle with facial recognition. Not the kind that unlocks our phones, where there is a controlled environment and we are looking directly at the screen. I'm talking about the kind where they have to pick people from a crowd instantly. For some reason, computers struggle to identify the most salient physical traits that make a person look like themselves.

Everybody from law enforcement to AI experts has turned to caricaturists to learn how they do what they do. Yes, the same kind of caricaturist who drew the embarrassing picture of you at your last corporate holiday party. Erik Learned-Miller of the Computer Vision Laboratory at the University of Massachusetts, Amherst, says that "the miraculous thing about caricature artists is that they're able to zero in on the most distinctive aspect of somebody." Learning to memorize names means we must learn to view people differently.

We all have similar compositions. Two eyes above a nose above a mouth. We are all way more alike than we are different, which is one of the reasons that it is easier to differentiate between people we know well. I know a pair of identical twins, and it was only after about a month of hanging out with them regularly that I could tell them apart just as easily as I could spot my other friends. Even though they are "identical," there are small physical variations to be found, not to mention differences in their demeanor and how they carry themselves. A caricaturist might pick up on these variations, and you should too.

When you meet somebody, ask yourself how a caricaturist might draw them. This can be a very uncomfortable experience if you aren't used to it. We are all taught to be polite, and for every person we meet whose strongest feature might be a chiseled face and strong jawline, there is another who may have a less flattering feature jump out at us. As we were taught when we were young, "Don't stare!" You should be able to identify a prominent feature quickly, and you can practice with people you see on TV or when you are out and about before you attempt it on the job.

Also, keep in mind that your ability to memorize names will quickly become something that others want to learn. Outside of suggesting this book, it might be wise to keep your imaginative imagery to yourself. Just because something is a useful tool doesn't mean that everybody will want to know EXACTLY how you are picturing them to remember their name.

Let's try a few right now. Look over the images below and see if you can find a way that you might caricature that person.

GRACE

ASHLEY

KEITH

Take a moment to think through your first impressions. If you were drawing a caricature of these 3 people, what would it look like? These are your own thoughts and don't need to be shared with anybody, so give yourself the liberty to use your imagination.

Okay, is it done? If you haven't done it yet, I highly recommend that you take a moment to try right now. You will get way more out of trying this yourself than by simply reading my choices.

When I look at Keith, the first thing that I notice is the shape of his hairline and how it makes what almost looks like a Batman logo. You may instead notice his beard right away, or possibly the caterpillar-like eyebrows. Like I mentioned before, it may feel strange to do this when, for most of our lives, we are trained not to focus too much on physical appearances. To do this well, it requires that we do the opposite of what we are used to, but keep in mind that this is all about an objective approach with a clear purpose. In no way is it about making judgments!

When I look at Ashley, the thin, descending eyebrows are the first thing I notice. One might also take note of your flower headband and matching top, but be careful about choosing objects or accessories on a person. If they change between meetings, your anchor could be lost at sea.

When I see Grace, I immediately notice the shape of her smile. She seems welcoming and inviting, and her cheeks frame the smile well. That's likely the section of her face that would be the most memorable to me and what I would highlight if I made a caricature of her.

It is far better to choose any feature than none at all, so don't worry if your first few attempts are tough to remember. It will get easier. I find that there are certain features that are far easier to remember for me than others. The first places I tend to look are always on their faces. It presents the most information and is the least likely to change from day to day.

Just like a caricaturist starts by learning to draw a regular face, you'll grow to start thinking of faces as rotating combinations of features.

- Eyebrows and Eyes
- Foreheads
- Lips
- Noses
- Wrinkles / Lines
- Moles / Beauty Marks / Dimples

If this seems overly simplistic to you, remember that all colors are created from only three primary colors. A beginning artist may only know how to make a single shade of green, but an established artist can differentiate between varying shades easily, adding or subtracting more blue or yellow to achieve the result they are looking for. Similarly, you will become adept as noticing smaller nuances that you may have missed before.

You can throw beards and facial hair in the mix as well, but those don't stick quite as well for me unless they are very prominent features (like Adam's beard). Accessories, like glasses and clothing, are subject to change, so those can be dangerous to choose as an anchor. In a pinch, anything is better than nothing, so it's better to choose somebody's glasses than to skip this step. At the very least, the extra effort put into noticing the person will go a long way toward remembering their name.

Keep in mind that these are designed to be temporary locations to hold information. Just like we don't have to use these tricks to recall the names of close friends and family members, the end goal is that eventually the names we learn become hard-coded into our memories through repetition, and we are able to ditch the mnemonics completely.

Remember that our working memory is very limited and can only hold about seven items MAXIMUM. This means that if you meet four people and have to memorize their names, that's already a taxing burden on your brain's processing power unless you use some kind of system. If you train yourself to look for identifying features, you are already a giant leap ahead, as you can better immediately differentiate the people you meet.

In Appendix C, you can test yourself on selecting identifying features to memorize a handful of names. I recommend reading the rest of this book, however, before skipping ahead.

# CHAPTER 5

# C2: CHOOSE A CODE WORD

Once you've identified a feature to CARICATURE, you're a third of the way through the 3Cs (remember: CARICATURE, CODE, CHANGE). The next thing to do is to choose your CODE word.

Your code word will be a word that you use as a bridge back to the name. Last chapter, we discussed Adam and his beard, and used the code word APPLE since it made us think of an "Adam's Apple."

If you have ever read anything about mnemonics, you may have heard of the "memory palace" technique. Essentially, it's the idea of using a place you know well, like your home, to function as a holding bay for information. Let's say that you need to buy five grocery items at the store: *broccoli, milk, chicken, yogurt, and flour.* You would take an imaginary walk through your home and mentally pin items at various locations. As humans, we remember pictures and stories better than anything else. Even thousands of years before the written word, we passed on information through stories and imagery.

For instance, as you walk up to your door, you might picture the doorknob as a giant head of broccoli. When you open the door, your kids have hung a bucket of milk above you that splashes down on your head and soaks you. In my house, I would enter a foyer, where there is an oil painting of my wife and me that was a wedding gift. In this scenario, our heads in the painting have been replaced by chickens! I would then move clockwise through the house. Notice that our piano is full of yogurt, and the keys have turned to yogurt as well. It's impossible to play anything without getting sticky fingers! Finally, I would see my dining table and notice that it was totally covered in flour. We have two cats, so I would even see their little paw prints in the flour as they chased each other.

Was that easy for you to picture? You may already be capable of running through the grocery list from memory. Without looking back, what was the doorknob made of? What happened when you opened the door? What about the big oil painting of me and my wife? And the piano? Finally, what about my dining room table? If you scored 5/5, congratulations. You're already a memory expert! If you didn't score well, don't be discouraged. Instead, take a second to really visualize the imagery and try again. By making these images stick out in your mind, you will eventually succeed.

This leads us directly back to code words. You already know what broccoli looks like, and most of us have a universal image that comes to mind. We need a different option for a name because we don't know specifically what a "Mary" looks like. Or what exactly a "Brian" looks like. If we did, all Brians would look exactly the same, and there would be no need for this book. You would just walk into a room and be able to identify all the Brians, all the Marys, etc. just as easily as saying "That is a book" and "That is a table." Remember that all a mnemonic aid does is function as a bridge leading from one piece of information to another. The code word is the bridge. When I think of the name Mary, the first thing that comes to mind is "Mary Had a Little Lamb." My code word for Mary is a lamb. For Brian, you might think of a brain, or maybe of Brian, the anthropomorphic white dog from *Family Guy*.

Unlike selecting an identifying feature, which is all about using visual cues, you will want to have the code words locked in pretty solidly for the system to work properly. Creating the caricature and applying a code word are your chances to be creative, so the word itself doesn't need to be another challenge.

You don't want to have to scramble to figure out what the code word is, so it pays to have them all memorized.

I've included lists of the top one hundred male and female names in Appendix A and Appendix B, but bear in mind that this list isn't exhaustive and only reflects the code words that I have chosen to be the most universal. They aren't always the code words that I use personally, and I'll explain why that is in a moment.

It doesn't matter much what your code word is, as long as it is something that you can remember. Unlike the variances that come with our caricatures, a given code word will stay the same for everyone sharing that name. Mary will always get a lamb. Mike will always get a microphone. Let's look at the people from the last chapter:

- Keith
- Ashley
- Grace

What comes to mind for *you* when you see these three names? Keep in mind, there are no wrong answers. For example, a friend of mine used to work for an animal rehabilitation center where they had a cheetah named Victor. Whenever I meet a Victor, I think of a cheetah. Nobody else would make that association, but that's okay. It works for me, and if an unusual association works for you, that's all that really matters.

There are some standard code words that have been accepted by the memory community at large, but your personal words and creativity will almost always be more memorable. You are looking for things that make you think of the name, so look for words or phrases that will instantly trigger that name. For the examples above, I use:

- Keith - "keys"
- Ashley - "ashes"
- Grace - "saying grace" (picture somebody saying grace at a dining table)

You can try a few more yourself:

- James
- Noah
- Brad
- Charlotte
- Mia
- Jacqueline

What does each name make you think about? If you want to, go to the name lists in the back of the book and see if the names that I provide match up with yours. If you prefer the code word that I have provided, feel free to go with it. Instead, you may discover that yours is more memorable because it is personal, and that's great too. There are no hard and fast rules, and the best code words are the ones that work best for YOU.

At this point, the hard work is almost done. You've picked an identifying feature on the person and identified a code word. If we think about it like the grocery list "memory palace" technique from earlier, the code word is the item on the grocery list, and the identifying feature is the location where you will pin the information. Now it's time to link them together.

# CHAPTER 6

# C3: CHANGE THE PERSON

Look at the picture above. Do you remember his name? If not, that's okay. Do you remember the funny picture that we made?

Do you remember what was in his beard? It's hard to forget the apples. If you don't remember the image, maybe you didn't picture it well, so go back and take another look. If you <u>did</u> remember the apple, but not the name (his name was Adam, like an Adam's apple), it's only because you haven't paired the code words with the right names yet. It's still a huge win for you. Correctly pairing the names and words is not very difficult to do, and you'll get there with just a bit of practice. I will give you some free tools to use in Chapter 8: Extra Tips.

When you CHANGE the person, you are going to affect them somehow with the code word. It is important that whatever you do to them touches them directly, and it's best to use an element of humor or exaggeration if possible, in line with thinking of the person like a CARICATURE. When we put the apples in Adam's beard, it's best to exaggerate. If we can create a story or additional context, it's even better. Maybe there are a ton of apples pulling his beard straight down, and that's why it hangs so long. Like we joked about earlier, maybe Adam secretly works for Apple computers, and his beard is weighed down by their logo. Maybe he is always looking for a healthy snack and keeps a few fresh apples in his beard just in case. The actual story doesn't matter, but it does matter that there is some semblance of a narrative, even if it's contrived and ridiculous.

Our brains remember pictures well, and they remember outlandish pictures even better. "It was the biggest fish ever!" "It was the tiniest puppy!" Nobody remembers things that fall within normal limits. When we make these pictures, we want to make them the biggest / smallest / least / most ever.

Now that you've seen how we brought this all together, let's go back to the people from the past sections.

First, we had Grace. As you may remember, we decided to focus on her gregarious smile. The code word was "Saying Grace" or maybe for you, it would be "Amazing Grace" (like the song). Just picturing her singing the song wouldn't be very memorable, but we can spice that image up a bit and make it something hard to forget.

Maybe we imagine that her teeth are the Twelve Disciples sitting around a table saying grace, and then at the end they all start singing "Amazing Grace" at the top of their lungs. The sound surprises everybody, including Grace! Now that's an image that would be tough to get out of our heads.

The code word for Keith is *keys,* and we looked straight to the shape of his hairline for the physical feature. We might imagine that Keith has a terrible memory for his keys, and so he has had twenty or so copies made of his house key. They are all on small key rings tied to his head by his hair, and they perfectly outline his hairline. Like I said earlier, if you haven't tried these kinds of visualizations before, they can be very daunting. They require you to unlock your own creativity and to give yourself permission to be silly, something many of us have forgotten how to do.

If you have young children, you've undoubtedly engaged your own imagination while working with them on their school projects. If they are writing a story, you may have helped them create characters or draw the monster antagonist. If you don't have children, you were once a child with an imagination. And if you feel like you've never had an imagination, it's probably time to try one on for size. Just because it's hard now doesn't mean that you can't do it. It only means that you are currently out of practice. The more you try, the easier it will become.

Finally, we have Ashley. The code word, as you may remember, is *ashes*. The first thing that I notice are her eyebrows. They have a specific shape to them and would be easy to spot if you approached her again. The flower headband would also be an obvious choice, but then you'd be sunk if she removed it. Now, it's your turn to create a story relating Ashley's eyebrows to ashes. Try to give it some context, and just for practice, see if you can come up with five different explanations. I'll give you mine in the next section, but you'd be doing yourself a disservice by not trying it first!

There is a certain knack for creating funny pictures on the spot, and much of that comes from letting your imagination run a bit wild. If you can easily come up with one explanation but not five, you might be holding yourself to the straight and narrow too much. There is a time to wear your analytical hat and a time to wear your creative hat, and right now it's time to temporarily shut down your internal auditor.

# CHAPTER 7
# TIME TO REVIEW

Before we talk about the importance of reviewing names, let's take a moment to go over a few ways to combine Ashley with ashes:

- It's her birthday, and while she blew out the candles on the cake, her eyebrows caught fire, and all that remained were the ashes. Luckily, the ashes stuck to her in a perfect formation, and nobody was the wiser!
- For fun, she decided to replace her eyebrows with ashes because it's the newest fad on Instagram.
- She is a devout Catholic and replaced her eyebrows so that she would be permanently prepared for Ash Wednesday.
- Maybe it's soda ash! She had very acidic eyebrows and brought the pH down by basting them in soda ash.
- Ashley wanted to have the healthiest eyebrows the world had ever seen. She read that controlled fires are good for the forest and thought, "Why would my eyebrows be any different?" She systematically burned off part of her eyebrows until only ashes remained, knowing that they would grow back even better than ever.

Obviously, these are ridiculous, but that's the point. In mathematics, $i$ is defined as the square root of -1. This is a number that doesn't exist anywhere in nature. Two negatives multiplied together will always make a positive. Although $i$ is imaginary, it is still useful in helping mathematicians solve complex problems. It is added to an equation and removed before the final answer. Similarly, the goal isn't to always picture ashes on somebody's face when you see them. It's to give you one small boost in remembering their name until it becomes hard-coded and something that you won't forget. Then, like the mathematical *i*, the image can be removed, and only the memorized solution will remain.

This brings us to the aftermath of reviewing our information. For whatever reason, you'll find that certain names and code words stick better than others. They may be easier to visualize, they may be more meaningful, or they may just be "stickier" for one reason or another. Others may be more fleeting. When you've had a chance to remember a small handful of names, step back for a moment and make sure to review the names that you have. Don't wait for 3 hours to check in on your images. A few minutes spent reviewing in between groups can be the difference between locking something in and completely forgetting it.

# CHAPTER 8
## EXTRA TIPS

## HOW TO PRACTICE

Take time to practice "when it doesn't count." If you are watching the morning news, use these techniques to memorize the names of the people being interviewed. While watching a movie, caricature the actors' faces and link their characters' names. Your goal in practicing is twofold: first, to memorize the code words so that they're available at the front of your mind, and second, to learn to quickly caricature the face. Eventually, it shouldn't take more than a passing glance to select your anchoring feature.

The best way to memorize the code words is through flash cards and something called *spaced repetition*. Essentially, you are quizzed on a small number of code names at a time, and the ones you struggle with or get wrong will appear more regularly than those that are easy for you. There is a free app called Anki that will make this easy for you, and you can download the app directly at https://apps.ankiweb.net/.

If you take a moment to register at https://kevinviner.net/remember-names/, you can get a free Anki file of all the code names in this book! Once you've downloaded it, you can sync it directly with your computer or mobile device.

As I mentioned at the beginning of the book, the best way to improve your memory is by making this a part of your daily routine. When you are at the grocery store, run through the 3Cs to remember the clerk's name. Try it with the flight attendant or with your child's classmates. You might find that once you start using people's names in conversation, they open up to you more and drop their guard. They feel better about their day. You may even find yourself playing the role of a REAL magician by changing the way that those around you feel.

# TIPS AND TRICKS

There are a few tricks that I've found to be helpful. When you stumble on a name that has an additional letter, you can use that letter to "brand it." What do I mean by that? Let's take two names, Mary and Maria. They sound similar besides the "a" at the end of the name. If you are Catholic, you may hear Maria and think "Ave Maria," picturing a choir singing it from their pews. Alternatively, you already know that Mary is a lamb, so to picture Maria instead, you can picture a lamb with a big A sheared from its wool. Similarly, Jim is a "gym" whereas Jimmy is a "gym with a Y," like the YMCA.

Some words require a compound thought. Something like Kimberly doesn't personally spring to mind a lot of thoughts, but Kim goes well with the code word *"Kimono,"* and the -ber part can be thought of as *"brrr..."* so you get *"Kimono Brrr ...,"* somebody wearing a kimono in the snow. Raymond becomes "ray mound," or a pitcher on the mound with rays of sun beaming down.

Finally, some names will use film characters or celebrities, provided that these associations are easily visualized. Benjamin becomes Benjamin Button, the movie character who aged backwards. Roger becomes Roger Rabbit, Donald becomes Donald Duck, etc. Once again, the most important thing is that it's something you can visualize.

Over time, you'll learn to add slight variants to the code words and their associated imagery. For instance, "Rich" might be cash flowing freely, and "Richard" might be thought of as "Rich-Hard," or "hard cash." Small variations like this will help with nuanced names.

# FOREIGN AND DIFFICULT NAMES

If you run into foreign or difficult to pronounce names, you are going to have to be extra creative in your assessment. It is sometimes harder to choose differentiating features on the face of somebody from another culture or ethnic background, and their names may use sounds or pronunciation that we aren't as familiar with. If you have a moment to look over the guest list for a class or meeting you are attending, you can spend a few moments in advance looking it over and familiarizing yourself with it.

Here are a few of the top foreign names worldwide:

1. Matias (France)
2. Constanza (Chile)
3. Katarzyna (Poland)
4. Beatriz (Argentina)
5. Mohamed (Belgium)
6. Olafur (Iceland)
7. Mitsuki (Japan)
8. Dmitry (Russia)
9. Abhinav (India)
10. Athanasios (Greece)

These are a bit harder, since we have no immediate attachments to most of these names. By using our imagination, we can start to create new associations. Just think of the names as a combination of sounds, and group them together. For instance, *"Matias"* could easily become *"My Tees,"* which would be thought of as somebody with a collection of T-shirts. For *"Beatriz,"* you could think of *"Bee Trees,"* which could be swarms of bees in the trees.

Spend a few minutes thinking about the names presented above and what your code words might be for them. Here's what I came up with:

1. Matias - My Tees
2. Constanza - Cannes Dancer
3. Katarzyna - Cat Arson
4. Beatriz - Bee Trees
5. Mohamed - Mohawk Med (doctor with a mohawk)
6. Olafur - Snowman With Fur (Olaf with fur)
7. Mitsuki - MIT Zoo Key
8. Dmitry - Dim Eatery
9. Abhinav - Ab in Half (like doing a crunch)
10. Athanasios - Athens iOS (like a new iPhone OS)

These are tricky and harder than the US names we are used to, but don't let that discourage you! You can do it, but it might take a bit more practice. If you come across a foreign name at an event, make note of it so that you can practice it. If you're aware of it, it is far less likely to trip you up in the future.

# CHAPTER 9
## WHAT'S NEXT?

When McDonald's added healthy items like salads to their menu, what do you think happened? Did people suddenly decide to eat healthier? Oddly enough, the opposite happened. According to a study from Baruch College in New York, one of our *cognitive errors* (like an optical illusion, but more of a mental illusion that affects how we think) is believing that tomorrow we will be more perfect than today. People thought, "I'll go ahead and order the salad *tomorrow*," so they chose a more unhealthy item in its place for *today*.

Try not to fall into the same trap with memorizing names. The best day to start practicing what you've learned is TODAY. The longer you put off starting, the less likely you will be to ever start. Practice in small doses, and realize that consistency over time will lead to improvement.

Remembering names is much more than a party trick. It's a way to create more lasting connections with people, and the focus required to properly caricature them and link the code word will force you to engage more. You may find that your confidence grows when you stop worrying about saying, "Sorry, what was your name again?" You may receive better service at your next appointment or meal. You may find that your employees respond differently to you, as knowing their names builds trust and rapport. You may even find that the creative exercise of making associations starts to open up other doorways into art, music, and other activities that you've eschewed in the past.

You might even woo your future spouse by remembering their name.

# APPENDIX A

## TOP 100 MALE NAMES IN THE USA

AARON - HANK AARON

ADAM - APPLE

ALAN - ALLEN KEY

ALBERT - EINSTEIN

ANDREW - ANT DREW

ANTHONY - ANTS IN HONEY

ANTON - A TON OF ANTS

ANTONIO - A TON OF OATS

ARTHUR - KING ARTHUR

BENJAMIN - BENJAMIN BUTTON

BILLY - BILLY GOAT

BOBBY - BOBBING

BRANDON - BRANDING IRON

BRIAN - BRAIN

BRUCE - BRUISE

CARL - CURL

CARLOS - CARLOS SANTANA

CHARLES - CHARRED O'S

CHRIS - CRISS CROSS

CHRISTOPHER - CHRISTOPHER ROBIN

CLARENCE - CLEAR RINSE

CRAIG - KEG

DANIEL - LION

DAVID - STATUE OF DAVID

DENNIS - TENNIS

DONALD - DONALD DUCK

DOUGLAS - DOUGLAS FIR

EARL - EARLY BIRD

EDWARD - SCISSORHANDS

ERIC - PRINCE ERIC

ERNEST - URN NEST

EUGENE - HUGE JEANS

FRANK - HOT DOG

FRED - FRIED

GARY - GARAGE

GEORGE - GEORGE OF THE JUNGLE

GERALD - CHAIR OLD

GREGORY - GREGORIAN

HAROLD - HAIR OLD

HARRY - HAIRY

HENRY - HENRY VIII

HOWARD - HOWARD STERN

JACK - JACK IN THE BOX

JAMES - GIANT PEACH

JASON - JAY SUN

JEFFREY - GIRAFFE

JEREMY - CHAIR EMMY

JERRY - MOUSE

JESSE - GUN (JESSE JAMES)

JIM - GYM

JOE - G.I. JOE

JOHN - PORTA-JOHN

JOHNNY - JOINT KNEE

JONATHAN - TOILET IS THIN

JOSE - HOSE

JOSEPH - TECHNICOLOR DREAMCOAT

JOSHUA - JOSHUA TREE

JUAN - WON (MEDAL)

JUSTIN - JOUSTING

KEITH - KEYS

KEN - KEN DOLL

KEVIN - HEAVEN

LARRY - CABLE GUY

LAWRENCE - LAW RINSE

LLOYD - LID

LOUIS - LOUIS VUITTON (BAG)

MARK - MARK ON HEAD

MARTIN - MARTINI

MATTHEW - MATT IN A PEW

MELVIN - MELT VAN

MICHAEL - ARCHANGEL, MIC SHAPED LIKE 'L'

NICHOLAS - ST. NICK

PATRICK - ST. PATRICK

PAUL - PALE

PETER - PETER RABBIT

PHILIP/PHILLIP - PHILIPS SCREDRIVER

RALPH - RALPHS GROCERY

RANDY - RAN DEEP

RAYMOND - RAY MOUND (SUN ON PITCHER)

RICHARD - RICHER

ROBERT - ROBBER

ROGER - ROGER RABBIT

RONALD - RONALD MCDONALD

ROY - ROY ROGERS

RUSSELL - POTATO

RYAN - RAIN

SAMUEL - SAMUEL L JACKSON

SCOTT - PAPER TOWELS

SEAN / SHAWN - 007 (SEAN CONNERY)

STEVE - STOVE

STEVEN / STEPHEN - STOVE OVEN

TERRY - TERRY CLOTH

THOMAS - TRAIN ENGINE

TIMOTHY - TIMOTHY LEARY

TODD - TOAD

VICTOR - VICTORY

WALTER - WALRUS

WAYNE - WAYNE'S WORLD

WILLIAM - WILL.I.AM (BLACK EYED PEAS)

WILLIE - FREE WILLY

# APPENDIX B
## TOP 100 FEMALE NAMES IN USA

ALICE - ALICE IN WONDERLAND

AMANDA - A MANTA RAY

AMY - AIM (TARGET)

ANDREA - SAN ANDREAS FAULT

ANGELA - ANGEL

ANN / ANNE - RAGGEDY ANN DOLL

ANNA - ANACONDA

ANNIE - LITTLE ORPHAN ANNIE

ASHLEY - ASHES

BARBARA - BARBED WIRE

BETTY - BETTING

BEVERLY - BEVERLY HILLS

BONNIE - BONNET

BRENDA - BRAND NEW

CAROL - CHRISTMAS CAROL

CAROLYN - CAROLING

CATHERINE - CATHERINE THE GREAT

CHERYL - CHAIR-OWL

CHRISTINA - CHRISTENING WITH AN A

CHRISTINE - CHRISTENING

CYNTHIA - SYNTH (LIKE A SYNTHESIZER)

DAWN - THE DAWN

DEBORAH - DEAD BOAR

DENISE - TIN KNEES

DIANA - PRINCESS DIANA

DIANE - DINE

DONNA - DAWN WITH AN 'A'

DORIS - DOORS

DOROTHY - BLUE DOROTHY DRESS

ELIZABETH - LIZARD BREATH

EMILY - FAMILY

EVELYN - EVIL INN

FLORENCE - LEATHER

FRANCES - FRANCE

GLORIA - OLD GLORY

GRACE - SAYING GRACE, AMAZING GRACE

HEATHER - FEATHER

HELEN - HELEN OF TROY

IRENE - IRONING

JACQUELINE - JACK-O-LANTERN

JANE - JANE FROM TARZAN

JANET - JAMMED NET

JANICE - JAM ICE

JEAN - JEANS

JENNIFER - GEMS IN FUR

JESSICA - JESSICA RABBIT

JOAN - JOAN OF ARC

JOYCE - JOIST

JUDITH - CHEW THIS

JUDY - JUDY GARLAND

JULIA - JEWEL IN SHAPE OF A

JULIE - JEWEL IN SHAPE OF E

KAREN - CARING

KATHLEEN - CAT LEANING

KATHY - CATTY

KELLY - EMMETT KELLY

KIMBERLY - KIMONO BRRR

LAURA - AURA

LILLIAN - LILY ANT

LINDA - LINT SHAPED LIKE 'A'

LISA - MONA LISA

LOIS - LOIS LANE

LORI - LORRY (ENGLISH TRUCK)

LOUISE - LOO ICE

MARGARET - VIRGIN MARGARITA (NO A)

MARIA - LAMB WITH AN A

MARIE - MERRY

MARILYN - MARILYN MONROE

MARTHA - MARTHA STEWART

MARY - LAMB

MELISSA - MOLASSES

MICHELLE - MY SHELL

MILDRED - MILD RED

NANCY - ANANZI THE SPIDER

NICOLE - NICKEL

NORMA - NORMA JEAN (CANDLE IN THE WIND)

PAMELA - "PAM" COOKING OIL

PATRICIA - PATRICIAN (NOBLE)

PAULA - POTLUCK

PEGGY - PEG

PHYLLIS - FLEECE

RACHEL - RAGE (OR RAID GEL)

REBECCA - TRIBECA

ROBIN - ROBIN (BIRD)

ROSE - ROSE (FLOWER)

RUBY - RUBY (GEMSTONE)

RUTH - BABY RUTH, BABE RUTH

SANDRA - SANDER (TOOL)

SARA, SARAH - SAHARA

SHARON - SHARING

SHIRLEY - SHIRLEY TEMPLE

STEPHANIE - STAY FUNNY

SUSAN - LAZY SUSAN

TAMMY - TUMMY

TERESA - MOTHER TERESA

TIFFANY - ENGAGEMENT RING

TINA - TINA TURNER

TRACY - TRACING

VIRGINIA - FUR GENIE

WANDA - WAND

# APPENDIX C

## YOUR TURN TO PRACTICE

Now that you've had a chance to review the names and code words on your own, it's time to practice!

Take a look at the following pictures of people and pick an identifying feature. Then look up the recommended code word for that person, or come up with your own! Finally, create a mental image to combine them together.

If you're reading a physical copy, I would encourage you to physically write in your answers. The more senses we can involve in our learning, the more likely it is that our learning will stick with us.

If you're reading the e-book version, be sure to take a moment to visualize your answers and think about them. Don't worry if you don't get them all correct. If you follow The 3Cs, however, I think that you'll surprise yourself with how many names you are able to recall!

**NAME: MICHAEL**

IDENTIFYING FEATURE:
(CARICATURE)

_______________________________

RECOMMENDED CODE WORD, OR YOUR OWN:
(CODE)

_______________________________

CREATIVE IMAGE:
(CHANGE)

_______________________________

**NAME: SHARON**

IDENTIFYING FEATURE:
(CARICATURE)

---

RECOMMENDED CODE WORD, OR YOUR OWN:
(CODE)

---

CREATIVE IMAGE:
(CHANGE)

---

**NAME: NORMA**

IDENTIFYING FEATURE:
(CARICATURE)

---

RECOMMENDED CODE WORD, OR YOUR OWN:
(CODE)

---

CREATIVE IMAGE:
(CHANGE)

---

**NAME: HAROLD**

IDENTIFYING FEATURE:
(CARICATURE)

---

RECOMMENDED CODE WORD, OR YOUR OWN:
(CODE)

---

CREATIVE IMAGE:
(CHANGE)

---

**NAME: JESSE**

IDENTIFYING FEATURE:
(CARICATURE)

---

RECOMMENDED CODE WORD, OR YOUR OWN:
(CODE)

---

CREATIVE IMAGE:
(CHANGE)

---

**NAME: REBECCA**

IDENTIFYING FEATURE:
(CARICATURE)

___________________________________

RECOMMENDED CODE WORD, OR YOUR OWN:
(CODE)

___________________________________

CREATIVE IMAGE:
(CHANGE)

___________________________________

**NAME: RICHARD**

IDENTIFYING FEATURE:
(CARICATURE)

_______________________________________

RECOMMENDED CODE WORD, OR YOUR OWN:
(CODE)

_______________________________________

CREATIVE IMAGE:
(CHANGE)

_______________________________________

**NAME: JULIA**

IDENTIFYING FEATURE:
(CARICATURE)

---

RECOMMENDED CODE WORD, OR YOUR OWN:
(CODE)

---

CREATIVE IMAGE:
(CHANGE)

---

**NAME: JOSEPH**

IDENTIFYING FEATURE:
(CARICATURE)

_______________________


RECOMMENDED CODE WORD, OR YOUR OWN:
(CODE)

_______________________


CREATIVE IMAGE:
(CHANGE)

_______________________

**NAME: ROBIN**

IDENTIFYING FEATURE:
(CARICATURE)

---

RECOMMENDED CODE WORD, OR YOUR OWN:
(CODE)

---

CREATIVE IMAGE:
(CHANGE)

---

**NAME: MARTIN**

IDENTIFYING FEATURE:
(CARICATURE)

---

RECOMMENDED CODE WORD, OR YOUR OWN:
(CODE)

---

CREATIVE IMAGE:
(CHANGE)

---

**NAME: SCOTT**

IDENTIFYING FEATURE:
(CARICATURE)

———————————————————————

RECOMMENDED CODE WORD, OR YOUR OWN:
(CODE)

———————————————————————

CREATIVE IMAGE:
(CHANGE)

———————————————————————

**NAME: ROSE**

IDENTIFYING FEATURE:
(CARICATURE)

---

RECOMMENDED CODE WORD, OR YOUR OWN:
(CODE)

---

CREATIVE IMAGE:
(CHANGE)

---

**NAME: ANNA**

IDENTIFYING FEATURE:
(CARICATURE)

---

RECOMMENDED CODE WORD, OR YOUR OWN:
(CODE)

---

CREATIVE IMAGE:
(CHANGE)

---

**NAME: PATRICK**

IDENTIFYING FEATURE:
(CARICATURE)

_______________________________

RECOMMENDED CODE WORD, OR YOUR OWN:
(CODE)

_______________________________

CREATIVE IMAGE:
(CHANGE)

_______________________________

**NAME: MICHELLE**

IDENTIFYING FEATURE:
(CARICATURE)

---

RECOMMENDED CODE WORD, OR YOUR OWN:
(CODE)

---

CREATIVE IMAGE:
(CHANGE)

---

**NAME: CAROLYN**

IDENTIFYING FEATURE:
(CARICATURE)

---

RECOMMENDED CODE WORD, OR YOUR OWN:
(CODE)

---

CREATIVE IMAGE:
(CHANGE)

---

**NAME: DENNIS**

IDENTIFYING FEATURE:
(CARICATURE)

---

RECOMMENDED CODE WORD, OR YOUR OWN:
(CODE)

---

CREATIVE IMAGE:
(CHANGE)

---

**NAME: LINDA**

IDENTIFYING FEATURE:
(CARICATURE)

_______________________________________


RECOMMENDED CODE WORD, OR YOUR OWN:
(CODE)

_______________________________________


CREATIVE IMAGE:
(CHANGE)

_______________________________________

**NAME: JANE**

IDENTIFYING FEATURE:
(CARICATURE)

---

RECOMMENDED CODE WORD, OR YOUR OWN:
(CODE)

---

CREATIVE IMAGE:
(CHANGE)

---

**NAME: PETER**

IDENTIFYING FEATURE:
(CARICATURE)

---

RECOMMENDED CODE WORD, OR YOUR OWN:
(CODE)

---

CREATIVE IMAGE:
(CHANGE)

---

**NAME: WALTER**

IDENTIFYING FEATURE:
(CARICATURE)

---

RECOMMENDED CODE WORD, OR YOUR OWN:
(CODE)

---

CREATIVE IMAGE:
(CHANGE)

---

**NAME: ALICE**

IDENTIFYING FEATURE:
(CARICATURE)

---

RECOMMENDED CODE WORD, OR YOUR OWN:
(CODE)

---

CREATIVE IMAGE:
(CHANGE)

---

**NAME: KEN**

IDENTIFYING FEATURE:
(CARICATURE)

---

RECOMMENDED CODE WORD, OR YOUR OWN:
(CODE)

---

CREATIVE IMAGE:
(CHANGE)

---

# TEST YOURSELF

Name:

Name:

Name:

Name:

Name:

Name:

Name:

Name:

Name:

Name:

Name:

Name:

Name:

Name:

Name:

Name:

Name:

Name:

Name:

Name:

Name:

Name:

Name:

Name:

# APPENDIX D
## SUGGESTED READING

**Books About Memory:**

*The Memory Book* - Harry Lorayne and Jerry Lucas

*Moonwalking with Einstein* - Joshua Foer

*Your Memory* - Dr. Kenneth Higbee

*The Mind of a Mnemonist* - A.R. Luria

*The Seven Sins of Memory* - Daniel Schacter

*In Search of Memory* - Eric Kandel


**Books on Creativity:**

*Thinkertoys* - Michael Michalko

*How to Write One Song* - Jeff Tweedy

*Drawing on the Right Side of the Brain* - Betty Edwards

# THE LINKING METHOD
## MORE FUN WITH YOUR MEMORY

Since you've come this far, I wanted to share a different memory trick that you can use for anything from grocery lists to studying for a test. The chain method of memory, also called the linking method, makes use of visualizations and images that are linked together one by one.

Let's take a list of 20 "objects." They may seem arbitrary at first glance, but I'll reveal their purpose in a few pages.

1) Teacup

2) Person Practicing Yoga

3) American Flag

4) Kneading Dough

5) Pack of Stands

6) Niger River

7) Brazil Nut

8) Man Banging on a Desk

9) Vodka

10) Sombrero

11) Ramen

12) "Eat the Pope"

13) Phillips screwdriver

14) Egyptian pyramid

15) King Kong

16) Vietnam Memorial

17) Persian Rug

18) Turkey

19) Oktoberfest

20) Tying Shoes

We are going to link each item to the next in the chain. It's important that these associations are strong because we are creating a continuous chain. As they say, chains are only as strong as their weakest link.

Begin by visualizing a Teacup. See it sitting on a table in front of you. We are going to affect each object by the object next in the list. It's important that they "touch" somehow. Ask yourself "What is happening to the teacup?" Somebody is practicing yoga inside of it! Make sure that you can see them in your mind before moving on. What do they look like to you? Are they tiny, or is the teacup huge? The more detailed you can make your mental snapshot, the easier you'll be able to recall it later.

What is happening to the person practicing yoga? They are wearing an American Flag, and it is being worn like a beach towel.

What happens to the American Flag? You are kneading red, white, and blue dough on top of the American flag to make patriotic 4th of July cookies.

You have so much extra dough that you need to place it somewhere. You notice a pack of music stands in the room, so you take the pack of stands and fill them completely with the dough.

The dough has melted all over the stands and you need to get rid of them, so you throw them together into the Niger River.

They all float down the Niger River together (they are in a pack, after all).

As you float down the river with the pack of stands, you hear Brazilian music start to play and a torrent of Brazil nuts falls from the trees above. The Brazil nuts are hitting you in the head.

Because the Brazil nuts are all falling into the river, the head of the nut company doesn't have any new product to sell. He is frustrated, and banging loudly on a desk to show his frustration. The water is amplifying the sound of the banging and it can be heard from miles away.

The man banging on the desk gets frustrated and turns to the bottle. It's a HUGE bottle of vodka, and he drinks it all in one sitting! The banging stops because he passes out.

Unfortunately, the man who drank the vodka passes out in the broad sunlight, so a kind passerby drapes a sombrero over his head to block the sun.

Those are the first ten. See if you can go through the associations yourself. I'll give you the first one:

1 Teacup

2 _________________

3 _________________

4 _________________

5 _________________

6 _________________

7 _________________

8 _________________

9 ________________

10 ________________

How did you do? If you didn't get them all, that's okay. Go back and make the associations more vivid in your mind.

When we left off, we had finished with a sombrero. You take it off the man's head, and you are shocked by what you see inside. It's filled to the brim with ramen, and you can smell the delicious tonkotsu broth.

As you finish the last of the broth, you are wondering what to eat next. There is a strange message written in the bottom of the sombrero, under all the broth. It's a picture of the head of the Catholic Church, and it simply says "Eat the Pope!" You don't know what it means, but then a voice starts in your head on repeat, almost like a broken record that keeps skipping. The voice is yelling "EAT THE POPE! EAT THE POPE! EAT THE POPE!"

The Pope is busy working on the Vatican, which is in need of major repair. Unfortunately, the only tool he has is a single Phillips screwdriver. He is trying to bang nails with it, and even to scratch new "art" into the walls using its tip.

Suddenly, this Phillips screwdriver grows to be HUGE, and the tip begins to resemble one of the great pyramids of Egypt!

On top of this pyramid is a gigantic ape. You look closer and it is King Kong! He has decided to take the pyramid as his own, and he is swinging wildly from its top.

You notice something else pointed besides the pyramid, and it is perched on top of King Kong's head. It's a *non la*, a traditional Vietnamese pointed hat, and it's the biggest you've ever seen! It's a perfect cone on top of King Kong's head.

Around the *non la* hat is a beautiful Persian rug. Its colors are bright and vivid, and the rug begins to speak to you! You've never seen a Persian rug speak before, and you ask it how it came to be here. It responds, "I Ran!"

Now we need to affect the Persian rug with a turkey. Simply seeing a rug with turkeys printed on it isn't unique enough. But what if the rug was made of Thanksgiving turkey? Hopefully you don't have pets, or the rug would be eaten within the week!

A little known fact about Turkeys is that they like to party hard. They are all drinking a hefeweizen beer at Germany's favorite celebration, Oktoberfest. Some of the turkeys drink too much so their gobbles become unintelligible.

And finally, what happens "to" Oktoberfest? In my mind, it is hijacked by people tying shoes together and throwing them high up on the power lines over the festival grounds. The festival is done, but thousands of people will be walking home barefoot tonight.

Your turn:

11. Ramen

12. ______________ (hint: what is the message under the ramen)

13. ____________

14. ____________

15. ____________

16. ____________

17. ___________

18. ___________

19. ___________

20. ___________

Now for the "surprise" part. I mentioned earlier that memory tricks are useful for studying. How long did this exercise take you? Maybe 15 minutes? In 15 minutes (or less), you have memorized the top 20 countries in the world in order of the largest population (as of 2022).

1: Teacup - China

2: Person Practicing Yoga - India

3: US Flag - USA

4: Kneading Dough - Indonesia

5: Pack of Stands - Pakistan

6: Niger River - Nigeria

7: Brazil Nut - Brazil

8: Man Banging on a Desk - Bangladesh

9: Vodka - Russia

10: Sombrero - Mexico

11: Ramen - Japan

12: Eat the Pope - Ethiopia

13: Phillips Screwdriver - Philippines

14: Pyramid - Egypt

15: King Kong - Congo

16: Vietnamese Pointed Hat - Vietnam

17: Persian Rug - Iran

18: Turkey - Turkey

19: Oktoberfest - Germany

20: Tying Shoes - Thailand

If you had to memorize these countries for a test, it would likely take you twice as long, and there would be no easy way to check in with yourself to make sure that your answers are correct. But as long as you make the associations vivid, you'll be able to picture them for hours. When you test yourself, the associations provide insurance that you aren't skipping anything! Your answers will always be right.

Whether you are getting ready for a speech, learning facts for a history or geography test, or helping your children with their schoolwork, the methods don't really change.

For items that need to be memorized in order:

1: Write a sequential list of the information that you need to know

2: Figure out "code words," or items that you can visualize that will cue your brain for the answer.

3: Link each associated item to the next in the list.

Have fun with this, and enjoy your newfound memory superpowers!

# ABOUT THE AUTHOR

As one of the top mentalists worldwide, Kevin Viner has appeared on Penn & Teller: Fool Us (CW), Johnny Carson: King of Late Night (PBS), Masters of Illusion (CW), Don't Blink (Pop TV), The Core (AMC), Busy Tonight (E!), and on Japan's Superdrama TV. He has consulted for finalists on America's Got Talent and has appeared in commercials for T- Mobile and for the film Now You See Me 2. As a corporate entertainer, Kevin has engaged top-level management with Starbucks, Google, Intel, Cisco, Ketel One, Deloitte, General Electric, and many more. He has worked with celebrities including Katy Perry, Alicia Keys, and Kim Kardashian.

Offstage, Kevin enjoys living life to its fullest. He is an instrument-rated private pilot, a marathon runner, and practices mixed martial arts. Along with his wife Jessica, Kevin is a songwriter and multi-instrumentalist. Their self-produced album After (h)Ours, released under the moniker Jessie Lark, was nominated for album of the year at the San Diego Music Awards. Kevin holds a degree in mathematics from the University of California, Irvine.

Follow Kevin @thekevinviner.